Praise for Stephan Silich

"Moments in time define, don't they? The split second, the muse and the making. And, how profound a split second can be. I love this about Stephan's writing; it really takes you into the corner of the photograph or fabric, whether that's the time of night, the moon in the sky out the window, or the number of steps on the fire escape. With each page turn in Stephan's book, I found the moment, place, and time."

—SARAH WRIGHT
Florist and artist

"Stephan is a true artist among us. I am at a loss to describe how talented he is and how his words touched my heart and soul. Go get this masterpiece. You will thank me and fall quickly for his work."

—JOSEPH D'AMICO
Owner and operator of All American Sports

"Be captivated by the wisdom of his poetry and his journey through the fragile times of adulthood and parenthood. Your life will be better for reading Stephan Silich's book."

—JERRY CAMMARATA
Author of The Fun Book of Fatherhood

"Each page, line, and word awakened all of my deepest emotions. I cried and laughed and found sadness and so much more with each heartfelt, unique poem. This very creative author leaves his personal imprint on these pages as he puts his precious view of life down on paper. Falling in love with this book of feelings was so very easy."

—AGNES VARONA OQUENDO
Author of Running Against Cancer, Nurse Diaries, Dark Whispers of a Serial Killer, and My Shorts

"Just as fabulous as the first book. So insightful and meaningful. It makes you question your own inner feelings and thoughts. Loved it. Stephan is a very talented and gifted writer. Thank you for this gift."

—LYNN KUENZLER

"Stephan has a true gift, and we are very lucky he has shared it with us. I loved every word of Stephan's book."

—JOHN SEERY

"I opened the book and was hooked immediately by Stephan's lyrical, deeply reflective, beautiful words. What a gift he has for expressing the human condition! While 2020 was a year of profound loss, Stephan was able to acknowledge the complexity of existence, transforming it all— loss and love and joy and sorrow, as well as daily observations—into a collection that resonates with the lives of those of us fortunate enough to read his words."

—SUSAN TAYLOR

"Hats off to Stephan. I like to read his words, but I usually go very slowly because his words relax me. His book is not something you read like a novel."

—DR. JOSEPH SUAREZ

"I am so impressed with Stephan's poetry. The wisdom coming from these pages is phenomenal. The book is a pleasure to read. It is so honest and creative that I find I have to stop and think about the depth of his thoughts. There is so much love in this book. What a gift he has! I couldn't put it down. Stephan has so much to say, and he is not afraid of emotion."

—MARION VITALE

"Once you open this book, you will not be able to put it down. I started and finished reading it in one evening and, quite honestly, words can't express how I feel. I laughed, smiled, and cried as I read every page. Just beautiful, honest, and at times quite inspiring."

—RENEE SCOSKIE

"Stephan has compiled years of life experiences into beautifully written short stories and poems. His words will make you cry, make you laugh, make you ponder life, and it will surely resonate."

—DR. BAHAR MALEZADEH

"We are both blown away by Stephan's writing."

—NOREEN AND SKIP LANE

"Absolutely magical! This book touched my soul. Stephan's writing has a way of making all of his words hit home."

—MARY ROSNER

"Keats, Yates, Wilde, Whitman, Bukowski ... Silich is right there with them. And to be honest, I feel more kinship with his words than with any of those guys'. The words are perfect."

—PAUL KUHN

"I must admit, I am in awe of Stephan's gift of being able to find the words (sometimes many, sometimes few) to transfer the depth of his thoughts and emotions about life's purpose in such a beautiful and sensitive way."

—JAY CHAZENOFF

"Stephan is a gentle and kind soul who sees life through a beautiful lens. The rest of the world is lucky to get a glimpse of life through his eyes and to see his inner thoughts."

—RONNI GUSSIN

"Stephan's words are incredibly expressive. They all seem to come out of childhood memories or present-day dreaming. Either way, they are exquisitely tender and earnest, inspiring, and beautiful."

—JULIA BRANDON

"What a beautiful book of poetry. I too am a native New Yorker and especially appreciated Stephan's sentiments about the city. A good reminder to look for the beauty in unexpected places. Definitely will be my new subway read for a while."

—JESSICA GUSHEE

"The poems are so beautifully written. The purity, simplicity, and beauty found in all that exists was so inspiring to me! The poems are raw yet uplifting and shed optimism and hope. Absolutely lovely read. Highly recommend!"

—DR. NAZISH ILYAS

"A gift of simple, beautiful poetry, filled with vulnerability and grace. Stephan writes about the joys of living life and paying attention to the simple, bare moments that we often rush past. Stephan slows us down and shows us the beauty and raw emotion in those moments. You feel your heart expand as the book unfolds."

—DR. JAME HESKETT

"This book is a brilliant piece of art filled with beautifully written words that take you down the bittersweet memory lane, inspirational, and so much more. An extraordinary collection, just as Stephan's first book was."

—RITU KUNDU

"Stephan's poetry has touched me. I just finished his second book, and it is wonderful. My favorite is '9 blocks.' I have 2 girls of my own and his words spoke true to what I have always felt in my heart. Stephan has a real gift and I hope there is more to come."

—DR. MICHELLE CAMMARATA

"My copy of 'tonight will be the longest night of them all' is never far from reach. I often return to these pages, seeking the stillness and comfort they awaken in me. Stephan Silich writes with open-hearted courage. The lucidity of his words, his humanity, and his sometimes-intentional vagueness are an honest offering to the soul as he entrusts his emotional life to language. His poetry left an impression of a deeply vulnerable beauty that blossomed and transformed quietly in my mind and heart. There is great joy to be witnessed in his words and great emotion to be heard in his whispered secrets if you listen closely."

—JENNIFER FONTAO

Also by Stephan Silich

The Silence Between What I Think and What I Say
BROOKLYN WRITERS PRESS (2018)

Tonight Will Be The Longest Night of Them All
BROOKLYN WRITERS PRESS (2020)

putting the trembling kiss at ease

stephan silich

BROOKLYN
Writers Press

Copyright © 2023 Stephan Silich

All rights reserved.
Published in the United States of America by the Brooklyn Writers Press, an imprint of the Brooklyn Writers Co. LLC.

brooklynwriterspress.com

Thank you for purchasing an authorized edition of this book and for complying with copyright laws. No part of this book may be used or reproduced in any manner whatsoever without written permission except in the case of brief quotations embodied in critical articles and reviews.

For permissions or information on bulk orders, please email:
contact@brooklynwritersco.com

TITLE: *Putting the Trembling Kiss at Ease*

ISBN 978-1-952991-20-2 (e-book)
ISBN 978-1-952991-29-5 (paperback)
ISBN 978-1-952991-22-6 (hardcover)

Library of Congress Control Number: 2024903949

1st Edition

Cover Design by Stephan Silich and Andy Semnitz

again...

for my daughters, emma and mia.
for my brother, robert.
for my parents, robert and dianne.

thank you for teaching me
to be a dedicated parent,
a loyal friend,
a faithful spouse,
and how to stay true and brave
yet tender and kind.

this will stay with me until the end.

and this will reaffirm
that i'm a better person
for having you all in my life.

i am overwhelmed to be
your father,
your brother,
and your son.

as always, this is for you.

"There comes a point in life, when you realize who really matters, who never did, and who always will."

Bench Plaque — Central Park, New York

contents

upon the death of my father	20
an homage to the art of love	24
conversation	25
waiting	26
for my little ladies	27
what's the point?	28
life and death	29
aged	30
the 5-minute poet	31
6 stitches	32
the clasp of her bra	33
after	34
mia	35
sunset and sunrise	36
the coffee shop	37
fatherhood	38
criminals	39
a job	40
time slipping	41
the worst weekend ever	42
the great ones	43
chew	44
millionaire	45
memories	46
rain on the way	47
the balustrade	48
summer in spain	49
they fail to realize	50
a life	51
into the sun	52
beethoven and bukowski	53
eyes open	54
freedom	55
the night's sky	56
the naked and the scared	57

the hummingbird	59
385 times	60
i know	61
vagabond reflections	62
summertime	63
quietness over vanity	64
victory	65
the passing of time	66
broken jar of jam	68
eyelids	69
red dress	70
tonight	71
majesty	72
my heart	73
tomorrow	74
waiting for...	75
until you find me	76
when you're coming and going	77
on the subway	79
defeat	80
the effort of the sun	81
those beautiful faces	82
the same time	83
sit on them	84
naked	85
most	86
gin and tonic	87
the 3-mile run	88
thanks, marcel	89
question #1	90
unburden	91
don't try to steal my crown	93
the ancient world	95
through my soul	96
the proust questionnaire	97
you	99
remembering	100
a father's eyes	101

the moon or the sun?	102
the revolutionary	103
forgotten	104
open window	105
i must move on	106
the woman in front of the mirror at the plaza athene hotel	107
new york now	109
truth	110
memories of big sur return	111
question #2	112
december's garden	113
the timelessness of you	114
traffic	115
mulberry street	116
survival of the fittest	117
remembering the way	118
a recollection	119
haunted	120
return to silence	121
prevail	122
the sad face of clocks	123
the strap of your dress	124
some things that help and hurt	125
a little and a lot	128
the white beach	129
brave	130
10:55pm, thursday	131
not today	132
i am still	133
no one will know	134
memory	135
urgency	136
measure?	137
the sweetness of your skin	138
dreams won and lost	139
a farewell speech	140
revelatory	142
success	143

blink of an existence	144
sometimes	145
straight through	146
one of the few	147
the american dream	149
perfect	150
well enough	151
the early hours of morning	152
saviors of art and life	153
hope	154
endurance	155
bad dream	156
the spaces between	157
back to life	158
hydrangeas	159
alone	160
no longer young	161
my aching hands	162
poem	166
rome	167
her hands	169
roll me in	170
the beginning and end of my day	171
alienation	173
whisper	174
catch	175
grace	176
blue	178
elizabeth street garden	179
truly alive	180
the familiar stranger	181
need	183
healing	184
who i love the most	185
time	186
toward her	188
untouched and touched madness	189
honesty	191

soho, new york	192
the bridges of paris	193
you	194
sleep	195
between me and the moon	196
unwrap	197
grasp my heart	198
timing	199
spring street station	200
Postscript	208
Isabel the Butterfly	209
The Ginormous Heart	210
I Walk the Beach with a Silent Friend	211
Shouts to the Angels Whether or Not They Listen	212
Acknowledgements	214
About the Author	216

upon the death of my father
(October 10, 1941 — October 28, 2020)

hey, dad, can you hear us?
are you ok?
how are you feeling, pop?

    "really good." (he whispers)

i say to myself:
it's going to be necessary to part now,
but i don't quite know how
because i never wanted to say goodbye.

hey, bob, i love you.
can you hear me, it's boo?
i love you.

    "i know." (he whispers again)

i say to myself:
beyond all achievement,
beyond all ambition,
beyond all work,
there is at his center of being
a loving, giving, kind spirit.

it was a life
that sprayed a vast array of light on many,
rippling across space and time.

and with that,
my mom holds his hand
and he manages to slip his index finger
out of her grasp
and place it just on top of her hand
as if to say
i am holding on,
ever so gently,
ever so lightly,

and i will let go,
ever so quietly.

i won't cause a stir for you.
let me go now, my dear.
let me rest, my darling.
let me sleep, my love.

you know how much i love to sleep.

yes — the long endless sleep
has arrived for you, dad.

and it's the crowning
of a good life,
a really good life,
your body of work,
your work of art.

your peaceful acceptance
leaves me breathless,
and it is what i will remember most.

your exuberance and happiness
was visible to us,
even when you were old and ill.

thank you, dad. i love you.

staring death now briefly in the eye,
my young soul is no longer young.

the honor and terror
of watching this is upon me.
the grieving has begun,
but my personal sorrow
seems accompanied
by the general sadness of humanity
during this time and year of 2020.
i know that everything we love —

people
and places
and things
will be taken from us.

but i also know
that the radiant imprints and memories
that these loves
leave behind
are permanently ours,
and this is the only permanence
we will ever know.

a radiance that will take generations to forget.

a radiance made brighter after learning
that the atoms of the universe
are endlessly recycled
and that the sun is actually a second-generation star.

a radiance made brighter
by the discovery
that human bodies are composed of stardust.

so it feels good,
very good,
to know that we all have
a little piece of the moon inside us.

i know that every obituary is a remembrance of a life lived,
but it's also an instructive guide to those still living.
so go forth with a proud step.

don't measure your wealth by the desperation of the poor.
don't measure your personal success by the failure of others.
don't cover your broken sensitivities by displaying hatred.

stay remarkably serene about the opportunities you lose
and the difficulties you have to weather.
remain bound by love and irreplaceable loss.

look for light,
however fading,
to shine through this bereavement.

the eulogy to your departed soul
is our intimate thread,
asking the attention of all around us
so that we can embrace a devotion we will never be able to name.

you were life's invisible made visible.
you were life's untouchable made touchable.
you were life's noble kindness to all living things.

and we are left now with whispers of immortality.

an homage to the art of love

the rain cleared into a june sunset,
and the ease of beauty arose
with its urgent imperfections
and the unalterable beat of your heart.

give me your gentlest thoughts
and let me regain some wistfulness,
because my words speak only of you,
alive with hope and lingering with possibility.

will i live to see this through?

will i live in the hearts of my daughters?

will i be left unreplaced in death?

i don't know,
but i will continue
through the strength of scar tissue,
always wishing i had the power to terminate the sun.

nothing remains.
i know that.
but i will at least die
in the name of progress,
and these realities of loss and sorrow
will keep us closer to home.

it's times like these,
when everything breaks,
that everything comes together,
and the art of love
shines through as an unyielding anthem to life.

conversation

young man: you never wanted to be an actor?

old man: no — not at all.

young man: why not?

old man: my tears are not for sale.

waiting

miss the train,
be late for the bus,
get stuck in traffic,
let the plane be delayed,

and then look around and
listen to the sound of waiting,
run into the silence of history,
look up and see the endless days
stretched out ahead of you,
prosaic and sprawling.

get a glimpse of the divine.
catch a fragment before it disappears.

shed your heart's blood to get there
if you have to.

give the promise of tomorrow.

watch cityscapes turn to dust,
the sea lose its horizon,
and the sky open without definition.

the bloom will bloom in earnest
to live the short life,
and the sun will set
as i listen to my daughters
laughing and running in the backyard.

for my little ladies

i can't do everything...
but i will do anything for you.

what's the point?

to make people feel less lonely, of course,
and to not be forgotten by those sooner
than you had hoped to have been forgotten.

all this madness
is from not being alone enough.

i know sometimes we only want
to see a sliver of the sky,
but this has been a place of atonement,
full of everlasting brilliance and bravery,
crushing the sustained weeping
and transience of human existence.

it is here
that we will find a way to hide something special.

it is here
where our life will become a memory
before we are even gone.

it is here
we will become the stories.

it is here
we will become the places.

and it is here
we will become you before we are even us.

life and death

life is finite from the start,
a series of near misses
marked by moments of hope
and small triumphs,
uplifting and heartbreaking,
with extravagant splendor
and astounding beauty in between.

a surpassing beauty perhaps,
standing tall,
caught between distance and memory,
with unblushing words of admiration,
graceful humor,
and intimacy.

our nights continue, unbounded.
our mornings breathe truth.

i hold you against my warm bones,
as we bow our heads and sleep with the night stars.

together we give meaning
to the passing hours,
speeding up
and slowing down
for no apparent reason
until these hours melt into future hours,
disappearing altogether
and yet remaining all together
with the evidence of our senses
and the element of our memories.

aged

i just read
an article
about pavarotti (who's 65)
and how he left
his wife of 36 years
to marry his 26-year-old
assistant.

it's a shame
he doesn't live
the way he sings.

the 5-minute poet

it was great coming out of that
expensive restaurant,
well-fed and over served,
thanks to my parents.

i climbed into
my dad's car
and he dropped me at
my apartment on 65th and madison.

i made it up to the 5th floor
and to the edge of the bed
when the phone rang.

she said
she was waiting for me
and would come right over.

i jumped up,
brushed my teeth, and
stared at the empty notebook,
knowing i had my next poem.

and so,
there i was,
waiting for the knock on the door,
feeling like a famous poet
for the next 5 minutes.

6 stitches

i would sometimes have to squint in daylight
to see her clearly
because all the beauty surrounding me
seemed to cloud everything.

i saw her through the cafeteria window.
i waved to her.
she smiled and waved back.

i kept looking
and ended up walking right into a low beam
at the end of the hallway,
which opened a cut above my left eye
that required 6 stitches.

she eventually left me
for a friend of mine.

they ended up happily married
with four daughters,
and i ended up with
a small scar over my left eye,
and a slighter larger one over my heart.

the clasp of her bra

there is
nothing
more exquisite
than
the woman
standing
in front of you
with
her arms
behind
her back
and
her hands
on the
clasp of
her bra.

it is as beautiful as time
sinking slowly between two lovers.

after

she
would walk downstairs
to the kitchen, naked,
and return
with a bottle of wine,
crushing
the century's tragedies
along the way.

nights like these
were made for the few.

mia

my little one,
always picking flowers
for everyone in equal measure.

i remember your birth.

the first grasp
the first smile
the first laugh

the newness surrounding us
and the incandescent light
that filled the room.

the irrevocability
of this beauty
created great love,
but also
the potential
for great loss,

a gravity that is solemn at times
and burdened by history.

this expanding galaxy of emotions
sharpens my awareness of humanity
and brings forth pure consciousness
of good thoughts and good deeds.

all you can do
is try and catch the light
as the seasons pass.

these exalted aims
will remain
as real as the poet's promise.

sunset and sunrise

the most important time of day
is sunset,
when you see the day that is gone
and ready yourself for the day that is coming,
a day that will break goldenly.

and you will have the privilege to honor
these first moments
with nothing but undeniable
possibility and nostalgia.

and every so often,
you will
need something
that will make these days less painful
and to find answers to some of these questions.

will you keep chasing a life that is always further ahead than sleep is behind?

will you keep running through the echoes of isolation and
past the edges of understanding?

will you slow this all down so you can let the present unfurl herself?

will you find the best season to appreciate the beauty of things?

and will you think of me often, as i do of you?

the coffee shop

sitting in that coffee shop,
a song comes on the radio
that reminds me of how love
was once capable
of drifting through these quiet spaces,
making its way through the lull between the stars,
and how it carried us
from here to there.

the room is no longer crowded,
the piano sits empty,
and the world is full of people
afraid to be alone.

stay pure and uncorrupted
among the winter of leaden skies,
and try to decipher these words
that i write for you,
which are carved in stone
and never written in sand.

fatherhood

i have become a father.

and all my thoughts are filled with a home
where the lights are on
and everyone inside is happy,
dancing
and singing
and laughing
and watching their children sleep
and their lovers undress
late into the night
as the stars whisper
somewhere between speech and song,
putting life back together
with every word spoken
and every song sung.

criminals

this is dedicated to the weak ones
who carry guns and knives
and travel in packs:

you never got me to beg.
you never got me to cry.
and you never got me down on my knees.
and when you tried ever so briefly,
it didn't end so well for you.

so in case you forget,
a man can be destroyed, but never defeated.

a job

one summer
i worked
with 2 guys from mexico
digging ditches for
swimming pools
under the
brave august sun.

it was just another job
like all the others,
until it came time to quit
or be fired,
and both felt just fine.

time slipping

these are my sweetest words for you,
and the saddest,
because everything
still carries me to you.

all that passes through my life
is but a verification
of time slipping away,
with the hours vanishing
before my eyes.

and this is still more beautiful
than i ever could have imagined.

the worst weekend ever
(*for emma*)

> *"daddy,*
> *that was the worst weekend ever."*

why, emma? you went to a birthday party on saturday,
and you had a play date on sunday.

> *"it was the worst because*
> *i didn't see you all weekend."*

and there it was,
11 simple words
that filled the sky
and allowed the moon to be seen
in its wholeness.

it is my tender salvation
and the exultation of existence.

the great ones

i went to the library
to read some books,
preferably the great ones,
the heavyweights.

but when i got there,
i was greeted sweetly
by the prettiest girl
i'd ever seen,
and i lost all desire to read anything.

so i guess some of the great ones were right
when they said:

> *"sometimes,*
> *even words fail."*

chew

on a plane back to new york,
i was reading a memoir
about greenwich village in the 1940s
while the girl next to me read a book
called ashes to ashes.

and then...
there it was —
so perfectly real and precise:
a 1-year-old boy
sitting in his chair
trying to eat the end of his sneaker
while it was still on his foot.

he chewed and smiled and chewed some more.

i was mesmerized by his preoccupation,
so i watched and took note

and then stared out the window,
realizing that when you dim the lights,
the picture becomes a little clearer.

millionaire

3:22 a.m.
watching
a boxing match
on t.v.
while flipping through
hunter thompson's the rum diary.

the city
is peaceful at this hour,
except for a few garbage trucks
loading up the day's junk.

i close my eyes
knowing
i will wake tomorrow
in the early parts of the afternoon,
like some drunk millionaire,
and return
to the haunting world,
where the continual struggle is
to remain a gentleman,
avoid the 9 to 5,
get a few words down on paper,
and have the better parts of life
cover the rest
as i wrap my arms around
the impossibility of being truly alive
in the midst of all these remarkably
beautiful and terrifying things.

memories

memories are untrustworthy—

but i remember you
and how you,
set apart like a star,
awakened humanity's consciousness
to see the wonders
of our planet,
our pale blue circle,
reflected in your eyes
and reflecting back into my eyes.

rain on the way

11:47 p.m.
i wait for the rumbling
of the subway tracks
and watch 2
middle-aged women
clean the platform
with buckets of soap
and wooden brooms.

for some reason
this makes me think about life
and the eventual end of it
and how i would like to go:

with my head down on the notebook,
pen wedged between my fingers,
tv off,
bottle empty,
symphony playing on repeat,
rain on the way,
and you sleeping next to me.

the balustrade

mountains speed by as we sit in your apartment
drinking wine and talking about girlfriends and boyfriends.

your handmade curtains hold their breath behind us
as we sit still with the last gasp of hope.

living this well past midnight, i stare at your mouth
but hear no words.

i walk out onto the balustrade
and take in the melancholy of these new york streets.

i close my eyes as this sea of agony
plunges into the throat of night.

the wine will run out and i will return home,
kneel over the empty bed and say a few prayers,
weeping into tomorrow because the sky above
will be a little less blue without you.

summer in spain

when i was 23,
i spent the summer
in spain
drinking with new friends,
running with the bulls in pamplona.
and going to bullfights in madrid.

we also visited
the world's fair in seville
and the olympics in barcelona.

the rest of the time was spent
in the mountains of toledo,
the restaurants of mallorca,
the beaches of san sebastian,
and falling in and out of love
as much as possible.

this
was the summer
to throw arms around life
and sleep tightly
in this heaven.

they fail to realize

rejection
is
the
victory.

it forces you to go
deeper,
to grab within
and show the earth
who you are.

this
continues
in writing
and in life
as
these
moments
turn words into pages
exuberant in spirit,
rich with humanity,
dense with detail,
and as fragile as your next breath.

a life

some lives are touched in a special way,
and the few, the lucky few,
live unassumingly richer lives,
and by richer i certainly don't mean financially.

their lives remain young throughout time,
fixed by success or failure,
constant through happiness and sorrow.

history will not record their voices,
but their voices will remain.

they will deal with those who seek out their weaknesses.
they will keep their sense of humor.
their outlook will be serious, but not somber.

they will retain horror for the fraudulent and deceptive
and follow their beliefs, regardless of career.

their mornings will begin with thoughtfulness,
and they will return home after work
to fill empty pages and blank canvases,
where they place the greatest amount of their souls.

this is the best they can hope for,
and it will bring astonishing triumphs
and stunning celebrations of life.

into the sun

tonight,
thoughts of you choke most of me,
but tomorrow
i will get out of bed
and walk straight into the sun.

these unhealed wounds
will be the redemption of my heart
as it unfailingly bursts with life
through the daily act of continuing.

beethoven and bukowski

1:34 a.m.
listening to beethoven's
piano sonata no.14
and wondering,
how many great ones
are really out there?

the critics never understand
that the work is not created for their review.

no marble was ever sculpted
in their honor and that's all you need to know.

but don't listen to the praise either.
that's the mistake that never stops being made.

instead, listen to that old poet
who said, *"believe you are good
when they tell you that you are good
and you are dead, dead, dead."*

eyes open
(for emma and mia)

i've seen
life at dawn shimmer
across the hudson.

i've seen men serve breakfast to the poor
before sunrise.

i've seen women hold families together
with indescribable tenderness.

i've seen children move their fingers
across the map of the world.

i've seen love float to the surface of sleep
when you least expect it.

and i've seen my daughters,
standing before me,
arms outstretched,
and they are too beautiful
for the world we live in.

the love i have for them
will be pondered by poets,
scrutinized by scientists,
and will remain
the most poignant testament of life,
shining through everything i have
and everything i am.

freedom
(may 2 1998, palm beach, florida)

there's a
great freedom
in anonymity
and in failure,

so avoid the masses
by staying in the trenches
as long as possible.

there are a lot of
traps in the world,
and there's always something about
popularity that will throw you a bit.

let them dislike you
if they have to.
it won't be from firsthand knowledge anyway,
so who cares?

i ask nothing of you all
except to leave me alone for a little while
so i have enough time
to finish what i've started.

the night's sky

there is wonder in this world,
and more often than not,
it's sketched on the night's sky
before the hours of morning.

there is romance that holds hands
with untampered emotion,
and there is value in your soul
because you make the life
of every living thing
more noble and more resplendent.

and in the middle of it all,
your beauty casts a glittering light
on everything in its path.

the naked and the scared

these words are not being written to sell anything.

i still believe that all art should be free.
the public has a human right to art.
it's for everyone. it's that simple.

so don't feel obligated to buy this book
or the other two i've written, for that matter.

steal it if you can get away with it.

i'm totally fine with that.

or borrow it from someone and photocopy the pages.

or go to the sad world of social media
and read some of the poems for free.

this author gets $1.87 per book (hardcover edition)
with a list price of $24.99.
i'm still not sure where the rest of the money goes.

so if you break it down,
that's $1.87 for the naked and $23.12 for the scared.

oh, you can also just send me a nice note telling me that you
love my writing, and i'd be happy to buy you a copy
and send it to you — free of charge.

i buy most of the books anyway
and give them away to whoever wants to read them.
i donate all the proceeds from the book sales
to my brave publisher so she can publish other
unknown and struggling writers.

maybe we can meet somewhere,
perhaps have a cup of coffee
or a glass of wine,

and embrace under the sun,
with these undulating words that should
bring us closer together,
which is the sole purpose of writing them,
and that shouldn't cost a thing.

the hummingbird

the world confuses
hype with achievement,
gossip with history,
money with culture,
and nationality with elegance.

all we can do is
keep an eye on the hummingbird,
join the celebration
of those who are
meltingly tender,
and follow the refined rhythm
of timelessness
and the contemplative gesture
of your undeniable presence.

385 times
(for pierre bonnard)

true love waits for us all
as we crawl out from under the sheets
and read about that painter
who painted his wife 385 times.

i know

i'm realizing now
that poetry
can weaken a man
as much
as the memories
behind the peeling paint
of apartment walls,
lost and forgotten along the way.

so the quest continues
to find dignity in one's solitude.

i am still searching
for the glory in that
because in the middle of most nights
when i can't sleep,
i still think of you.

vagabond reflections

live life
as anonymously as possible,
like the ones who
built the world's great cathedrals.

let others
angle for the spotlight
and swallow lies and attention
like cold glasses of water.

believe in
vagabond reflections
of life and art.

believe
in the poet
who writes his words
on napkins in a bar.

believe
in the artist
who brushstrokes subways
because he can't afford a canvas.

and believe
in the hours of night
when there are things
you can't believe are happening.

these are the things one must
live with silently.

and so i choose now to be silent.

summertime

love must have another name
because this blue summer crushes
the drunk symphony dreams
of young men and women
reading lazy winter poems
on garden benches.

quietness over vanity

i have no comment,
and i hope they realize
that there is something noble
about just sitting in a room
and saying nothing.

just sitting there,
feeling the day,
and being quiet.

victory

lying in bed,
staring at the ceiling,
and thinking about the sad faces
in heavy-framed pictures
and how the peacefulness of a room
is ruined by false laughter.

i'm still aching from the sight of you
and from the way you hold your coffee cup.

i never thought i'd make it to even 30,
and yet i'm well past there,
and this is my small victory.

the passing of time

time is all there is.

don't let the hateful ones pierce you.

move past the unfeeling ones,
the perceived normal ones.
their judgements hold no weight.

act with consideration.

pause and take a moment.

care about the possibilities.

avoid the medications that prolong
and refine the suffering.

don't celebrate the history of the privileged few.

selfishness is not a virtue.

altruism is not a sin.

keep your dreams unfolding,
your work unfinished,
your life imperfect.

there is sweetness in the air,
if you know where to look for it,
pure and divine,
like the slow beating of your heart.

face the hard truths:
cells mutate and death shakes the earth.

get behind the meaning of every word
and the essence of all things.

have a light touch with everyone.

opt for presence over achievement.

stay suspended between youth and adulthood.

unlearn all that you've learned.

wrap your arms around the dignity of childhood.

move away from the cities
and those poisonously obsessed with status.

disregard the pretentious glass walls and luxury towers
that surround us with pristine mediocrity.

the only benevolent kings are the stars above,
and remember,
there are more stars in the galaxy
then there are grains of sand on earth.

there is a clear message in impermanence,
in the inevitability of decay,
in the necessity of togetherness,
in the value of restraint,
in the nostalgia of absence,
in the sincerity of privacy.

pay attention to the silence and the sustenance.

be abundantly modest.

listen to the voiceless.
the faraway things are just as important.

let the ashes of memory linger,
and our hushed ceremonies
will mark the passage of time
as gracefully as possible.

broken jar of jam

just last week,
a woman walked past me with the same
perfume my ex-girlfriend wore 25 years ago.

i haven't thought about her once since that time
and yet, when i smelled the air,
i instantly had to push back tears.

how long does it last?
how long before all that is hidden resurfaces?

and how long does love remain
the broken jar of jam
on the kitchen floor?

eyelids
(for emma and mia)

i dream as i walk
with my daughters,
energetic and noisy,
past the museums
and landmark buildings of the upper east side.

i watch their smiling faces
and hear the excitement in their voices
and the vibrancy in their hearts.

untroubled,
i have a newfound respect
for the protective covering of my eyelids.

and the greatest privilege in life
is now mine.

red dress

the woman in the red dress
with the red shoes
on the old cobblestone streets of rome
just smiled at me
as she stood in front of the hotel...

and the world is a good place.
i am sure of it.

tonight

i write these lines
and sing these blues.

i do this to keep your face from fading
and to leave
a human note,
a benediction,
and a meditation
on the unbearable weight of enduring love.

majesty

what is paramount
are the words and paintings
that keep us from dying
because
the ability to recede
is part of the gift of life,
which must be filled
with art and poetry
that always returns your love
back to me
with a little added majesty.

my heart

i sit here and briefly weep
because in this cruel world,
my heart still drools for you.

tomorrow

after the rain,
the flowers try even harder.

and i will try harder
not to lose anyone that carries my history
and to continue with the hunger in my heart,
which remains untouched by time.

my kiss to you
will always be given
with all the magic
and sweetness capable
from one human being to another.

waiting for...

waiting for the woman
i want to marry
to turn the corner,
i feel the
sidewalk shake,
and i am stunned
by the elegiac shocks of beauty
from every part of her.

she is a song,
and she was written just for me.

until you find me

i will try to
cover the distance between us,
and i will
hide you in my arms
while the earth turns...

until you find me
hiding in your arms.

when you're coming and going

i moved to a new apartment,
2 blocks from the old one.

this one has an outdoor terrace,

which i happen to be sitting on
as i write this,
drinking wine
and listening to the rhythms
of the air-conditioners from
the surrounding buildings.

the sky is a bluish-grey, and
i can actually make out a
few stars.

i am alone and
it is quite wonderous.

i love these apartments —
the small rooms,
the worn carpets,
the cracked paint,
the leaking window,
the dishonest landlord,
the drunk super,
the insane old ladies,
the miserable old men,
the scared and the pathetic,
the hysterical and the mad,
the misplaced and the forgotten.

no one really speaks
to each other in the elevator
or passing on the stairs,
and no one really says goodbye
when you're packing up
and moving out.

it's just the human soul,
magnified,
put under the microscope,
tissue detected, but not diagnosed.

it's just the way it is

when you're
coming and going
through this life,
these moments,
these fragments,
these haunted faces
with eyes closed to the burning minutes of life.

but it is also the crucial gift
of showing you the humble details
which gain more meaning than one thought possible
with each passing day.

on the subway
(october 17, 2020)

sitting on the subway
thinking of her

as the centuries
flash by
one stop at a time.

defeat

i've always believed that
a certain amount of defeat is necessary,
but not too much.

so when you're sitting alone
in your room
watching the floor dry,
it's important to know that
hope is the best of things.

and it's not only hope,
but love,
and the memory of love
that sustains
and is never forgotten.

the effort of the sun

heading down the fdr drive
on a monday morning,
i noticed a stretch of the east river,
shining proudly.

the fog was crawling north to south,
with patches of clouds,
and there stood the sun,

trying
and trying
and trying

and it was then that i realized,
just the effort was enough.

and this reminded me of you
and how your smile defeated decades of sadness.

and i still ask myself,
will you stay with me?
will you be my love?
will you let me fall at your feet,
not deferentially, but intimately?

and will you let me think of you
in the passing of my years,
generously and abundantly,
with the unexpectedness of stars?

those beautiful faces

don't let them fool you.

they didn't earn them,
and there's really nothing to them.

the american obsession
with youth and beauty and fame
destroys the margin
between life and death.

for the unwritten,
underside of history
has taught us that
popularity negates authenticity.

disregard it.

dedicate yourself so that
your capacity for feeling
overwhelms
the simplicity of everyday life.

disregard the culture of winning
and individual success
wrapped with self-centered ambition.

it is the most disquieting
thing about humanity.

look for kindness.
she will wait for you.
and when you find her,
everything will have its value.

and it will be a joy that does not seek more.
it will be a joy that rests,
satisfied,
at peace,
a joy that is full.

the same time

i can only hope
on some nights,
you will think of me,

and on some nights,
i will think of you.

and with a little luck,
these thoughts
will occur
at the same time,

and what had once been lost
will now be regained.

sit on them

the writing
occurs
in a
small room
in a building
off a rundown street

where i
spend many hours
fighting
with
life and
literature
by making small books
of poetry
that you can stick
in your back pocket
and sit on them
from time to time
if you feel like it.

and just maybe
with a little luck
some of these words
will anchor
our existence,
and reading them
will be a small victory
of what it means to be alive
and of what it means for hope
to finally be at rest.

naked

everything
comes down
to
this
moment,

this
bed,

this
bottle of wine,

this
song,

and
this
light
slipping through the curtains,
bouncing off your face onto mine.

most

it is you that i miss most,
and yet you are still here.

gin and tonic

as
the
years
burn,

i
finish
my drink,
throw
the empty glass
off the terrace,
and lift my face
to the sun.

the 3-mile run

a few nights a week,
i jog up madison avenue
from my apartment on 65th street.

i run 30 blocks and back.

on my way up,
i pass this burger place.

i always know
i'm close
because i can smell the grill
and grease in the air.

i love passing it,
not just for the smell
and thoughts of sinking my teeth
into a cheeseburger,
but because of
the cashier in the front window.

she usually doesn't notice me,
but i notice her
and her casual stance
and the way she briefly interacts
with customers.

there is an easy way about her
that instantly turns
these new york streets
into pure harmony
as i run away
into the early evening
with a newly acquired wisdom
not even the great philosophers
can provide.

thanks, marcel
(for mom)

i've tried reading
proust's
remembrance of things past
on several occasions,
but i've never been able
to get through it all.

which is actually
of little importance
since the only thing
that stayed with me
was marcel's ability
to write about how
he would wait,
with literal
breathlessness,
for his mother's
goodnight kiss.

and if that's
what i remember most
from his writing
or from the love of a son for his mother,
then that's certainly
a more reasonable importance
than anything else
i can think of at the moment.

question #1

have you ever noticed,
and i mean really noticed,
how so many essential
and meaningful things
emerge from people
who aren't
fully accepted
and embraced
by society?

unburden

her face
stayed with me
for the rest of the day
and into the night,
giving me
a strange sense of hope,
knowing that
just seeing her
could unburden the lingering
of this lazy summer day.

which reminds me
that when someone you truly love dies,
you should wake up the next day
and feel lucky to be alive.

yes, you will be heartbroken
and yes, you will be disillusioned
that someone can just disappear
without your having any idea where they are,

but you should now want to stay alive
make love,
make music,
write words,
paint paintings,
cook food,
stare at the moon,
weep at the stars,
walk next to the sea,
climb the mountain,
ride your bike,
take a bath,
and embrace it all
because there is strength in needing others,
and because you have a choice in how you respond.

and you will not languish.
you will prevail,
and you will flourish.

don't try to steal my crown

this
is my song
yet
to
be
sung.

so please don't try to steal my crown
before it's won.

i am
aware
of the
intricate and delicate
system
of
lies
we are supposed to follow,

and like the caterpillar,
i will do all the work
and the butterfly
will get all the glory,
but i wouldn't want it
any other way.

with
no seatbelt
and no helmet,
i'll travel to
wherever it is i have to go
because there will be more stories.

there are always more stories.
and even if we are no longer in the foreground
of each other's lives,
we can stay in each other's background for decades
and be full of wine,

and stay in bed together
with the windows open
the music on repeat,
and us, full of inspiration,
and love,
and hope.

the ancient world

you
must remain
faithful
to the
memory of your 1st love.

it is
more
beautiful
than
the burning tips of cigarettes

and
the body of christ

and
the sun hitting your face
through a nearby window

and
picasso's *guernica*

and
saint jude

and
even
those moments
that are
so perfect
they make you weep,
crushing humanity's discontent
along with the strange sorrow
of the distance of time
on a broken planet,
shuddering and floating
through a familiar stillness
straight toward a reclamation
of our infinite and unbounded love.

through my soul

walk with me
and let's pass the small cafes
that keep us together,

the open windows
that let us spy on our neighbors,

the desperate fire escapes
that let us stay afloat above ground,

the comforting sidewalks
at the beginning of day,

the brave stones
of our bridges and museums,

the concrete
on the shoulders of those who thrust
this city upward,

and these buildings
outside our doors
that surround time and memory
and continue to fill everything
with a fullness that
passes between us
like the silence of history
while we try to hold on to
what always seems to be slipping
through our fingers.

the proust questionnaire

what is your greatest fear?
that love is not enough.

which historical figure do you most identify with?
the caveman.

which living person do you most admire?
my mother, my father, my brother, and my two daughters.

what is the trait you most deplore in yourself?
none.

what is the trait you most deplore in others?
narcissism, selfishness, snobbery, cheapness,
and the general crudeness and unkindness of people.

what is your favorite journey?
walking my daughters to school every morning while holding their hands.

on what occasion do you lie?
very rarely, but if i do, it's to not
embarrass or hurt someone.

what do you dislike most about your appearance?
everything and nothing.

which living person do you most despise?
lawyers, politicians, dmv offices, ticket writers, and most actors and models.

what is your greatest regret?
i have no regrets.

what or who is the greatest love of your life?
my daughters, emma and mia.

what is your current state of mind?
breathless...always slightly breathless.

if you could, what would you come back as?
i'm not sure i'd come back.

what do you consider your greatest achievement?
my 2 daughters, failing as a married couple, but succeeding as parents and friends, not allowing myself to be defined by an occupation, never bowing to anyone and never letting bullies get away with anything, completely loving someone outside my family, and maybe a few written poems, a few taken photographs, and a few cut pieces of wood.

what is your most treasured possession?
my childhood.

what do you regard as the lowest depth of misery?
the subpoena and the lawsuit, the general crudeness of our american cities, followed by the parking ticket and the new york city landlord (and of course, divorce court).

where would you like to live?
anywhere there are artists, kindness, and an ocean nearby.

when and where were you the happiest?
sleeping close enough to hear my daughters
breathing in the next room.

what is your favorite occupation?
spending all my time with my 2 daughters
after that maybe some reading, writing, photography, and some carpentry.

who are your heroes in real life?
florists, painters, writers, musicians, teachers, carpenters, children, sanitation workers, police officers, and the united states military.

how would you like to die?
shark attack, motorcycle accident, trampled or
gored by a bull, plane crash, blown up in a war,
or perhaps just quietly in bed right after making love.

what is your motto?
protect yourself at all times and come out fighting.

you

you
are
my
howling
muse
declaring
war
against
all
limitations.

remembering

is
so
much
more
beautiful
than
forgetting.

a father's eyes

i don't know
if you've ever looked into the eyes—
i mean really looked into the eyes
of a man who has just lost a child—
but if you have, then you know.

> *"i'm sorry we have to meet under these
> circumstances... i don't know what
> to say except maybe try and focus on
> those great things you remember about your
> son—those things that made him your boy."*

he straightened himself and
suddenly appeared 2 inches taller.

> *"indeed. indeed. thank you."*

he continued:

> *"you know, i'm one block from the ocean
> in pompano beach — please
> come visit me sometime —
> we'll have a drink and watch the sunset."*

i told him he had a deal,
put my hand gently on his shoulder,
and headed straight for the exit.

the moon or the sun?

many say the moon looks so lonesome.

i disagree.

it's the sun that is so gloriously alone.

the revolutionary

someone asked me once how i would like to die,
and i recalled reading a story about leon trotsky,
the marxist theorist,
and how he was killed in mexico.

he was stabbed with an ice pick
but didn't die right away.

he was bandaged up and taken to his lamenting wife.

they retreated to their bedroom
and made love all night.

he died first thing in the morning.

that was it.

perfect.

a pure shot of beauty.

a revolutionary to the end.

forgotten

by
the
time
i
will
have
been
forgotten
by
the
world,

i
will
have
hopefully
forgotten
you.

but
the
durability
of
love
will
prevail.

open window

i leave the window open
in order to catch the morning light
that drapes your back
and starts the beginning of day.

in that, there is permanence enough
to crush the old cities
and obliterate every standing cathedral
known to man.

i must move on

lying in bed with her,
smell of salt rising from the beach,
night moon giving life to the night sea.

she gently tucked her head
into my neck
and occasionally rose to
kiss my cheek.

and the last time,
she moved her mouth toward
my ear and said:

> *"i would love*
> *nothing else but*
> *to stay here with you forever,*
> *but there's*
> *another world out there for me,*
> *and i really have to go.*
> *please forgive me."*

and just like that,
she was gone.

i never saw her again,
and that was 32 years ago,

and my heart remains
exquisitely forgotten.

the woman in front of the mirror at the plaza athene hotel
(from 40 east 65th street #5b)

sitting on my apartment terrace,
i unknowingly glimpsed
into the half-shuttered window
of the hotel across the street
and saw the side of a naked woman
moving toward the bathroom mirror.

she sat on a white bench
and lazily brushed her hair,
over and over again.

seeing her there,
framed against the new york sky,
i searched wistfully
for the meaning
and found that this was
just one of those moments
shining through,
like a brilliant, burning ray of light.

and this was all i needed
to get through the next couple of days.

we ended up looking at each other
until she gestured for me to call her.

she held up her fingers and spelled out the numbers.

i called and invited her over.

we put on some music, drank some wine,
and stayed together on the terrace
and under that hotel window for the rest of the day.

we went for a walk a little later,
and i dropped her off at the hotel.

the next morning she was gone,
and as i looked up at her window,
the white shade was pulled down,
and in red lipstick across the back
were the words:

    "thank you, my afternoon love."

new york now

as rents rise,
streets suffocate,
the individual
becomes
invisible,
and the skyline remains
dangerously elegant.

the developers elbow
and push from behind
like the bullies they are,
crowding out the ones
who were here in the first place,
with perfect indifference
to the comforts of others,
which of course leads to the desolation
and isolation
that lingers,
even as the sun brightens.

the city has gone
from a place of promise
to a dream deferred
as i ask for an occasional
moment of respite
in the midst of these days and nights,
filled with hallucinatory musings
of hopefully better things to come.

truth

all the things my mother
told me in my blurred youth
are about to come true.

so i will continue
performing small tasks
with quiet concentration
as my heart pulses inconsolably
amid a world
driven by perpetual change
and inevitable loss.

but i will also
keep the rare gift
of remaining as hopeful as possible,
because where love is,
death will never come.

memories of big sur return

the architecture of the mountains.
the design of the stones.
the tranquility of the waves.
the redemptive roadsides.
the half-built landscapes.

finding the divine here
requires absolutely no imagination,
so i will continue
with sweet, driving youth,
unselfish freedom,
and the emphatic understanding
in the choice of goodness.

question #2

why are beautiful faces always the ones
that seem to be the saddest?

don't they know that hearts are kept with tenderness?

don't they know that somewhere there are children at play,
pure heroes among us?

don't they know that words matter?

don't they know that illness and time catches up to all of us?

don't they know that there are only a small number
of star-filled nights?

and don't they know that in the vast expanse of space,
the moon will always be our guide?

and finally,

don't they know that it's the certainties of love
that always prevail?

december's garden

the moon sighs
on the most glorious night of summer,
and we are alone
like the old always are.

where is this so-called saint of our times
defending the war of love?

i know there's a little death in every tear,
but i made peace with this years ago.

i know we suffer most in order to heal,
and we heal by the memories of once being held.

i know our songs of hope
are also the cruelest of the season.

but i know this is also the season
that the flowers seek apologies
in december's garden.

the timelessness of you

the crudeness of modern life
is crushed by the timelessness of you.

traffic

in the middle of the day,
once in a great while,
the traffic seems to disappear,
if only for a moment,
and you can actually hear
the wind through the trees.

and between that space
there are the unvoiced lamentations
of lost innocence,
and unbridled devotion
to places and heritages,
to the briefest of interludes
to the bravest of revelations,
all unfolding slowly,
without diminishing any of our dreams.

mulberry street

standing on mulberry street,
with the moon to the left,
the empire state to the right,
and you in front of me,
before my eyes,
before my dreams,
before the foot of new york,
drenched in nostalgia
for a vanishing city.

this is my ballad
of longing
turning into love,
turning into solace,
and turning into endurance,
lingering with ease,
trying to finish the unfinished,
and walking a longer distance
straight to the closeness of our intimacy.

survival of the fittest

i survived a gun to the back of my head
and the trigger pulled.
i survived another gun put to my face,
with the threat of the trigger pulled.
i survived 11 bullets shot through my car windshield.
i survived the punches and kicks of three men at the same time.
i survived a shark swimming into my legs in juno beach, florida.
i survived running with the bulls in pamplona.
i survived riding a motorcycle for 8 years without a helmet.
i survived the unfulfilled promises of unrepentant love.
i survived the death grip of greedy bosses.
i survived the cruel lies of the nightly news.
i survived the incessant talk about weather and traffic.
i survived the narcissism of gyms and the self-posing selfies.
i survived the twin evils of finance and real estate.
i survived the desperate displays of 5-inch heels,
and i survived the memory of that unknown girl,
on that unknown street,
in that unknown city,
at that unknown hour.

and rather than fold my arms to the night,
i searched for my spirit
and was granted a sense of clarity,
pushing through the heartbreak,
the terror
the disquiet.

i keep my eyes open now to see
what i'm not expecting.

and my heart,
straining with tremulous beats,
still rises above the struggle
to hold on to
the fragments of these verses
that once spoke to you only
and that will speak to you again.

remembering the way

on the precipice of euphoria
with an exquisitely delicate memory...

i am remembering the way things move on,
the way things disappear,
the way things come back,
and the unrecorded moments
that shape our lives.

the awareness of all this impermanence
can be the great blessing of your life,
because understanding the temporal nature
and the sheer fragility of everything
should lead you to live your life like a prayer.

the gift of this day
and this long golden sunlight
will represent all the gentleness in this world
and all the tribulations of our bursting hearts.

a recollection

if you were here,
i would ask you to walk with me
to the sea that flows into the rocks.

i would ask you to let time
stand still between us,
the way it always did.

i know i will leave this life
facing the sadness of this loss,
but i will try to cover it with more love.

i know i will remain ever wistful.

i know i will live through our existence.

i know i will reap the benefits
of having known you
and having known your value.

i will keep you forever in my recollection,
half-hidden in the flickering candlelight.

haunted

i remain
haunted
by the same happiness
that infused
all the memories
of our years together.

when your strength comes back,
or when the wine starts her magic,
i will be dreaming of your love
and writing about it for years to come,
because true art is created with kindness,
and because we are here
to see one another through it all.

yes, we may be damaged
but by no means broken.

it is not lost on me
that for every abomination in this life,
i can still name a moment of grace.

return to silence

a weight has settled on me,
a disappointment without definition,
which i hope will serve to heighten
my sensitivity to all things,
instead of destroying
the tenderness gained.

i fought through
wars to reach
this moment,
only to have it slip away
with the longest goodbye
anyone should ever have to endure.

though i will continue to spend
many hours of many days
dreaming of you,
i know at some point
everything returns to silence.

prevail

sometimes the moment finds me,

my hands tremble
the sky becomes irrelevant
bewilderment becomes unfailingly unrestrained.

with all the days
still to come,

i know
i will somehow
triumph over this life,
despite the vagaries
of an uncertain future
and the never-ending search
for a glimpse of a much more peaceful life.

with this,
my soul is slowly being inhabited
by the daydreamer i knew as a child.

though there may be
a mournful hint to my eyes,
it is only because of the failures
and imperfections
that we succeed.

and this success is nothing more
than the simple results of an unfinished life.

the sad face of clocks

when i was in grammar school,
i would stare at those oversized clocks
in the back of the classroom,
the ones that don't move for some time
but then,
as you're sitting there
thinking it's broken,
it suddenly jumps ahead 5 minutes,
without warning.

i always found those clocks
to be terribly sad.

just the thought of them
fills the night air
with the unfounded loneliness
of an unrealized dream.

especially when
you think about
the importance of time
and how under her watchful eye
there are some people
getting up and getting ready
and others
giving up and moving on.

the hushed grace of time
and its haunting intimacy
are all we have.

the strap of your dress

all of my sorrows
cannot lift the moon from the mountains,

but after seeing
the strap of your dress
slipping off your left shoulder,
my hope emerges, reluctantly,
for one more kiss
that will surely crush
the inherent tragedies of life.

some things that help and hurt

the heroic pursuit of love.

the look for the soul in the forlorn.

the strain of melancholy in your words.

the evening that lets the stars nourish you.

the world you will not let defeat your goodness.

the urgency of these words for you.

the many great things that i just don't want.

the belief that what is not widely visible is always most beautiful.

the echo of undiminished daylight.

the way that certain unspoken things linger over everything.

the waking up with a calm i cannot explain.

the omissions and absences that fill the record of your life.

the restless heart beneath the vast sky.

the extreme sensitivity to aliveness that we call beauty.

the splendid, realized childhood.

the elusive feeling of poetic inspiration.

the emotional swells of existence.

the epic fall and the spirit's triumph.

the near past bringing remembrance of things further past.

the elegance of expressing the inexpressible.

the unsung struggle that brings a resignation of muted aspirations.

the nature of memory and the shades of recollection.

the darkness you settle into at night with filtered hope
from the streetlights outside your window.

the reassurance that something can be safely left behind.

the promise of steadying yourself in these staggering times.

the long, hard road that will have to be taken slowly.

the joy caressed with a bit of sorrow.

the wondrous fullness that comes during a father's watch
over his child's midnight sleep.

the light that is unlensed and unbent, bringing nothing but illumination.

the celebration of the people we engage with along the way
through magical nights unspoken.

the enduring need for us to gather together and listen to stories of love.

the sky that hangs every refrain and is ready to burst at any moment.

the dedication to those who lose their way across the sweep of life.

the wistfulness and lyricism of memory's capacity.

the surviving and the bearing of witness to all
that is delicate.

the howling, by way of the heavens, that reaches into the hearts of generations.

the music that simply makes life bearable.

the devotional language of children, the language of simplicity,
the language of absolute sincerity.

the tribute to your mother's and father's hopes.

and the day all your dreams are awakened,
unfolding over time,
coming back into a love that never goes away.

a little and a lot

no matter how much i thought of the things
i needed money to buy,
there was always that something unknown that pushed,
or rather guided me,
in the complete opposite direction and toward
a little madness
a little poverty
a little obscurity
and a lot of privacy.

this way of life may be perceived as not so serious,
but perhaps laudable to a few - a very few though,
or perhaps none at all - which is, either way, irrelevant.

it's also slightly unsettling at times,
but there is a pleasing disharmony and incompleteness
that makes the complexity of life bearable.

peace of mind will absolutely be reachable,
but there will be moments when the day breaks you
with its brutality and anguish,
and there is nothing you can do about it
but stay loyal to the dignity of humankind.

remembering to disregard
the unending journey of never having enough,
avoiding the reality shows, the tv, the movies,
and the nightly news,
the biographies of the wealthy,
the glossy magazines, and of course,
the car and beer commercials.

time will bring out the truth and dissolve all else.

so whether ignored or noticed,
remain unshaken at all times,
because true beauty is always found
in the parts you cannot see.

the white beach

i am dreaming of
long days
and the undying graciousness
of the gentle surf beyond the white beach.

you looked as pretty
as i have ever seen you.

your hair fell loosely
to your shoulders,
your eyes were slightly tired,
and your face was damp with sweat
from the afternoon sun.

and all we did
was laugh happily,
searching for a few answers
on this overwhelmingly
decent,
very decent,
summer day.

brave

if you're
brave enough
you can find
a world unto your own

where you
weep at the morning sun,
close your eyes to the wind,
sleep in beds you always make,
marvel at the magic laughter of children,
burst your bursting heart
at the very sight of her,
and take in all these moments
that will never disrupt
your sense of amazement.

and all the elements of richness
that keep you looking fondly on the past
and eagerly into the future
will allow everything around you
to smell like the night's stars.

10:55pm, thursday

i glimpse her
in the back of a taxi.
our eyes meet,
and she eases a smile toward me.

she betrays me
with words i never hear
but leaves me
feeling human again.

not today

it may be tomorrow,
next week,
next year,
or the next lifetime,
but just not today.

and so there will be
no regrets
for the time gone
and for the things left unsaid.

let's just leave it as
the inevitability
of impermanence.

the ache will remain,
the tears will continue,
and no one will ever know
what it means to lose you
except me.

i am still

i am still dealing
with words that once said love
but never meant love.

i am still counting
the times when something comes up
during the day
that i want to share with you.

i am still learning
that you are important enough
for me to worry again.

i am still looking
for that small window of time
when night replaces day.

i am still breathing
a more exalted air
because of you.

and i am still hoping
to conquer the coming day
with the courage you give me
in the middle of each night
when you wrap your arms around me.

no one will know

looking upon the end
as the sun dims
and the glaciers advance.

the last flower,
the last river,
the last breath,
the last touch,
the last blink of time.

the luminous fragility
that awaits us all
will arrive for me.

i will not fight one minute of it
because no one will ever know
the immeasurable splendor
i have already experienced
because you are my parents,
because you are my brother,
because you are my daughters.

memory

i eat when i'm hungry,
i sleep when i'm tired,
and all the rest is you.

you are my grand gesture
against hard fate.

everything matters when it comes to you.

i will continue to feel this way
right up until the very end.

every word i write is nothing more
than a fight against time.

everyone i love is nothing more
than a war waged against the world.

i cast these private truths
in a single ray of sunlight
because i want an honest witness
to the glory and mercy
that comes with taking this all in
as if each day was truly my last.

urgency
(april 30, 2019)

i turned 50 a few months ago,
and the yearning and anguish
hasn't diminished one bit in mid-life.

though i am at peace now
and see beauty
in almost everything,

whether the lushness of a rain-filled afternoon
or the stillness of a warm weekday evening,

i simply find inspiration
in the uncapturable urgency of existence.

measure?

how do i measure my love for you?

the same way one measures
the whisper of the wind,
the angle of the shadows,
the light of the moon,
the vastness of the ocean,
the temperature of the sun.

it is impossible.

so crawl into my arms, my little ones.

i will always be here for you.

the sweetness of your skin

that lingering scent
is the remnant of my memory
of our being together.

tenderly,
my eyes remember you,
and the more i look at you,
the more stunning you become.

the allure of you
still makes me feel
weightless in your arms.

and because of this,
there is no way
i'll ever be able
to say goodbye,
because all i long for
is your undeniable presence.

dreams won and lost

listening to your breathing
through the night
teaches me that anything worth knowing
should be closely observed.

i watch you two little ladies
sleep with a soulful gentleness,
and i realize that
painting has its brushes,
ballet has its techniques,
music has its notes,
writing has its words,
and love has the heart,
which always determines
which dreams are realized
and which are forgotten
in the wonder and wonderment
of all our days.

a farewell speech

above all,
be capable of feeling deeply.
this is the most noble of all virtues.

never be afraid,
especially when death comes.

the courage displayed
will slow things down for everyone
and allow the details to be illuminated
the way they should be.

let this light be welcomed
as you realize that
a single moment
is sometimes more important than a life story.

the words you've cried
have reached a caring few.

happiness in one way or another
is attainable,
despite the frailty around us.

you hold on to the things you love
because they are indeed withering in front of your eyes.

that should be enough.

that should be enough
for exalted love
by all,
for all,
with all.

but it often isn't.

and that disappointing devastation
will be the one thing you need to overcome
to get through the bareness of life
and live alongside time as it runs out.

revelatory

look twice at the girl
sitting alone in the coffee shop.
she just may be the one.

say hello.
tell her your name.
ask her what her name is.

go for dinner.
go for a walk.

talk to each other.

share music.
share words.

hold hands.
hug.

find the grace
to choose togetherness,
despite the unknown.

and when the day grows dim
under our planet's only sun,
your revelatory love
will be preserved and sustained
with great deliberateness,
and the gasping recognition
of this crowning glory will be yours.

success

just
because
something
ends
doesn't
mean
it
was
a
failure.

blink of an existence

look at
the anonymous faces,
the anonymous names,
the anonymous streets,
the anonymous bridges.

look in the old windows of closed shops.

remember your first kiss.

hold each other the forgotten way.

find rest in this unresting place,
find beauty in the creations
that are greater than the cruelties,
find hope in the triumphs that outweigh the tragedies.

how does the world look to you?

on this end,
it's to be embraced
because on less good days
you are there to make the most
of these intervals
between waking and dreaming.

in this blink of existence,
bookended by nothingness,
it is your simultaneous
presence and absence
that hurtles me through life,
past the ungenerous ones
and straight to the rarity
of our elusive
and unfiltered love.

sometimes

it's
the shape of your feet
and the bottles of old wine.

it's
the curve of your neck
and the undiscovered cobblestone streets.

it's
the way you hold a glass
and the empty rooftops.

it's
the thought of the kiss
rather than the kiss itself.

it's the intrepid sun, trying in late january.

and sometimes
it's as simple
as watching you in the bath,
soap running over your stomach,
hands resting on your sides
while buildings sleep,
stores close,
and the moon reflects
our sacred exaltations
of being here
and staying right here
in this moment.

straight through

these words,
this music,
these paintings,
and your eyes
carry me
straight through
the breathlessness of humankind.

one of the few

i saw you
standing
in the street
as it
rained,

the same rain
that has
fallen
for a
thousand
years.

you are closer
far away,
and
my ability
for a little
undisturbed
peace
gives me
renewed
awareness
of the
promises
of life.

and these words
i write for you
bring me
extra breath.

there
are
only
a few
happy men

in this
world,
a very few,

and i can
assure you
that i am one of them
because of you.

the american dream

we continue to occupy
hours on the phone,
days in front of the television,
weeks staring in the mirror,
years pretending to be happy,
decades at dead-end jobs,
and centuries dreaming
the lost hope of our childhood.

look past it.

run with the hunted.

break the bones of life.

strive for something virtuous,
like the first attribute of beauty,
luminous and hushed,
shining venerably
through everyone and everything.

close your eyes to see the light,
and then open them to the revelation
there is no other life than this,
and that is enough.

perfect

i've always believed that
a certain amount of defeat is necessary,
but not too much.

so when you find yourself alone
on nights like these,
it is important to remember that
hope is the best of things,

small miracles still happen,
and the perfectness of these moments
will let us thank the gods
for letting this hold in place
just long enough.

it will be possible
to ride this straight through the fire
and have our words of love
become the last recorded testament of humanity.

well enough

there has been
cheap wine and radio music,
hysterical lies and complicated betrayals,
great arguments and not so great dissolutions.

but there have also been
those nights,
those many nights,
which no words could match.

i wouldn't trade that
for anything in the world.

the early hours of morning

i feel so much better looking at you,
and it's nice to feel this way,
especially when you know it's the little things:

the glimpse of your eyes briefly catching mine
or the small birthmark on the side of your neck.

you are my beautiful accident,
the one i dreamed of
but never expected,

and it almost broke me
before our breathless beginning.

even your absence
fills the empty spaces of night,
like the moon showing herself
for a brief moment
just beyond the church rooftop
in the early hours of morning
in late january.

saviors of art and life

they paid
179 million for a picasso
157 million for a modigliani
324 million for a dekooning
469 million for a davinci
284 million for a cezzane
210 million for a gaugin
200 million for a pollack
183 million for a klimt
186 million for a rothko
194 million for a rembrandt
110 million for a basquiat
142 million for a bacon
100 million for a warhol...and on and on...

these saviors of the art world,
the so called preservers of culture,
are the same ones who
never work in factories
never sweat in kitchens
never do their own laundry
never go grocery shopping
never make their beds
and never properly love
their wives and their children
(though they do love their dogs).

they have slowly murdered life,
and now they do the same to art.

hope

i watch you walk past me
and hope you turn around
and hope you come back
and hope you think about me
when you return home
and lie down
on your side.

i wish i could call you and tell you
that love isn't something that weak people do.

love is pure and gentle,
and together it takes an awful lot of bravery.

endurance

let that something
rise up
in your heart
and whisper

if it's forgettable,
then forget it.

if it's loveable,
then love it.

and if it's endurable,
then endure it.

bad dream
(for emma)

did you have a bad dream, emma?

> *"sort of, daddy.*
> *i was crying*
> *because i'm not*
> *going to see you tomorrow.*
> *does that count as a bad dream?"*

that counts, emma.
in the sweetest way possible,
that counts.

the spaces between

still trying to discard
possessions and not amass new ones.

ridding myself of anything
and everything nonessential.

i've been doing this now for 30 years
because i realized very early on
that it's the spaces between
where one makes a life,

it's the quietness in those spaces
that speak louder than any words.

back to life
(for emma and mia)

let me touch your
still-sleeping faces.

you're in my bloodstream
and beyond.

you're in the sun by day
and the stars at night.

you breathe me back to life
with simple harmonies
of softhearted words.

this is the measurement of a good life,
and this is what leaves a lasting mark.

hydrangeas

over the last 18 years,
i've planted over 150 hydrangeas
in the backyard of my home
in the springs of east hampton, new york.

after my latest planting,
i sat on the couch
and paged through a book on the language of flowers.

i looked up the definition
and it said their meaning was:

> *"it's over but think well of me."*

and that sums up my first 50 years on this planet.

so this is a small thank you to the plants
and the soil
and the water
and the sun
that taught me
to stand still when you can,
with great interludes of calm,
and watch the truth of love
rise and remain,
fall and disappear,
and rise again.

always rising.
always remaining.

alone

be careful,
the crowd is gathering,
and that means
mediocrity is being properly assembled.
stay away from it all.

the worst is not being alone.
the worst is not even death.

it's death before death.

it doesn't have to be a short life,
but we make it short
by not paying attention,
by being distracted and preoccupied,
by running to achievement and ambition.

stay away from it all.

even if every exit is blocked,
there is always a way to conduct yourself.

believe me,
my eye is on the exit.
it's always on the exit.

take thought.
have devotion.

and live by the imperishable wisdom
of always following
the sweet sounds of your beating heart.

no longer young

i am surrounded by
my children's drawings
and pictures of my family
from a more certain time.

i let these memories float
among the endless days before me.
i have seen what few men have seen,
and yet i still haven't given in to despair.

what remains
is a delicacy
known only to the aging.

it is a dream many times dreamt.
it is refined simplicity.
it is undiminished purpose.
it is the strength of kindness.
it is the revelations of understanding.
it is the gentleness in words.
it is the brushstrokes of promise.
it is the forbearance of austerity.
it is the irrevocability of time slipping away.
it is the slanting sun yielding to the night,
reminding me of forgotten innocence.

it is the resoundingly
and unreservedly
well-written love story,
the ancient one,
the one told through the ages,
the one that contains the beginning
and the unwinding
of our exalted existence.

my aching hands
(for emma and mia)

the delicacy of your births,
which seemed at once
extraordinary and ordinary,
echoes constantly through
all i understand and experience.

the beating hearts
that weren't there a minute before
still astound me.

you are our tributes to humanity,
and every coin in every fountain
is a wish for you both.

believe what you can.
hold on to what you can.
the human condition is not an easy one,
so don't be numbed by routine.
try not to talk about the weather or traffic.

the law of nature should never leave you:
everything that lives will die,
and at some point
there will be no more hope for continued life,
and this should guide all you do.

be grateful in a way
that only someone who has lost
what you have lost can be.

the flowers
are sweeter
because they are short-lived.

keep your awakened sense
of what it is to be in this world.

walk barefoot on dirt,
on sand,
on stone,
on grass,
on snow,
on water,
on wood.

be careful of the greedy ones
and a few others not worth mentioning.

for many,
lying is the only way
to get through the day.

you can feel sorry for them,
but don't follow them,
don't acquiesce to them.

avoid the self-interested
and the strange posing rituals
of the obvious and desperate.

don't be at the behest of others who don't know you.
forget their reactions and especially their opinions.

money and fame are actually the opposite of success.
don't praise them. don't chase them.

be kind to each other and to yourself, always.

talk about your specific concerns
and your sorrows and hopefulness.

shrug off the expectations of youth and perfection.

leave them with words that soar through the air,
and if not words,
then a piece of art
or the touch of your hand.

be romantic, but never cynical.

be prolific, but not opportunistic.

don't take yourself too seriously.

don't take yourself too lightly.

make time to think and dream.

be the ones who smile at strangers
on crowded streets
at the end of an exhausting day.

keep your ceaseless ability
to see beauty in all people.

never deny the indisputable gift of your existence.

become part of wilderness,
not a part of a scene.

become part of the wind
that scatters your spirit.

suffer for
your aloneness,
and for bruising more easily,
crying harder,
remembering longer,
and feeling more deeply.

for you stand still and strong,
like stones through rivers and over sand.

and lastly,
remember,
always remember,
that my aching hands,

in my old age,
and even when i'm gone,
are for you to hold
at all times.

poem

    write
        a
           girl
              a
                  poem
                      and
                          she
                              runs
                                  away.

rome

the romance of possibility
where the past shines on,
forgotten treasures of a forgotten city.

these monuments of life,
museums inside and out,
provide a respite from daily life.

they remain
under stone archways
and tree-shaded terraces,
around vine-covered courtyards,
and whispering fountains,
outside workshops and store fronts,
underneath handmade rugs,
and alongside craftsmen,
paper makers,
and book makers.

and you and i alone
with unfaded pleasures,
trading kiss for kiss.

with things to do. more things to do.
with things to come. more things to come.

our faces grow older
around sad eyes, but we're not sad.

we know
the gods
in time
will ask for us,
and we will
fold up the moon,
put away the clouds,
and sweep up the stars.
but before the drowsy

calm of life catches us,
we will sleepily reach for the light switch
and dream of being great souls
in another world.

her hands
(*for mia*)

on saturday mornings,
we would walk across
the warm beach
and climb the sand dunes.

through the white patch of tall grass,
covered with sprinkles of purple flowers,
you would laugh
and say, *"it tickles, daddy,"*
and then hold my hand tighter.

i held your heartbreakingly small hand
for as long as you would let me.

it was there that i discovered
how to be a father,
with these reminders of humanity
all around me.

to you, mia,
i look to find meaning,
to reach truth.

please keep your tiny hand always within reach.

you will always find mine waiting for yours.

roll me in

when the time comes,
just dig the hole out back,
wrap me up in some burlap,
and roll me in.

toss some dirt on top,
and maybe plant a flower or two.

i hope you don't find the words too hard to say
to this spirit born of earth and water,
because words are all we have,
and love is the sweet sign of the divine
for us all.

the beginning and end of my day
(for dad, september 10, 2020)

walked my daughters to school this morning,
and we passed the local flower shop.

we stopped in front to smell the terracotta pots
filled with basil, mint, thyme, parsley, peppers,
and strawberries.

the lovely ms. sarah came out with a few pieces of rosemary,
rolled it back and forth in her hands,
and gave it to my daughters,
explaining how it increases the smell.
both emma and mia put a piece in their schoolbags.
we said thank you and continued on.

i dropped off my littlest first.
she kissed me smack on the lips,
gave me a big hug and said:

> "daddy, i love you
> to the moon and back,
> a hundred million times".

off she went to play with her friends
around a small doll house in the back of the class.

i dropped off my oldest, and she kissed me on the cheek
and said, "have a good day at work, daddy,
and don't cry when you say goodbye."

this made me think of my father
and how i fought back tears every time
i said goodbye to him for as long as i could remember,
starting back in high school, around 16 years old.

just last month
i received a copy
of his latest brain scan,
which indicated 2 new lesions.

a disease he has been fighting
in earnest now for 3 brave years.

i gave him a call on my walk to work
and said:

> *"dad, thank you for fighting this,*
> *and for hanging in there. it means a lot*
> *to me and to your little granddaughters.*
> *i love you. i hope you know that."*

and without missing a beat,
he said:

> *"i love you too, son.*
> *you have no idea how much i love you —*
> *as much as your daughters love you:*
> *to the moon and back,*
> *a hundred million times."*

we both laughed, thinking of emma and mia.

i laughed a little longer,
trying to postpone the tears
that were already on their way.

alienation

the
alienation
of
the
artist
thankfully
continues.

whisper

what
will
be
the
words
you
whisper
when
you
turn
toward
the
last
moments
of
a
very
good
life?

catch

the frayed edges
are surpassingly delicate,
so don't promise too much,
or you will risk
having something with less meaning.

when the shadows grow long,
don't leave.

when the sorrows are deeply planted,
don't let go.

not even the flowers
can bring back the lost songs of innocence.

we can still catch this at the right moment,
whether in late sunset or early dawn.

the forward motion of our time
leads to only one destination.

this has already been
more splendid than i ever thought possible.

grace

the way you hold your head
with a slight tilt
when you're listening.

the way you place your hand
on the side of your cheek
when you're thinking.

nothing but grace, freely given.

the simplicity of two people facing each other.
the rarity of two people listening to each other.

i know full well
how much loneliness there is in the world,
from love or no love,
and i don't want to be parted from that anymore.
i want to feel everything.

the things we carry,
haunting echoes,
unrelenting melancholy,
are all left behind with unsung exuberance
because your eyes season everything.

you will be my final expression.
you will be my last hiding place.

these words hold on
to the edge of my lips
as i wait for you to return to me.

i know the answers are always the questions,
but in every fragment of meaning,
there is you.

the filtered sun through these windswept trees
is specific to a certain hour of day,
and this hour is upon us.

keep it just like this.

blue

the blue light from the night sky
filled your bedroom,
surrounding us with memory,
distilling and refining
and slowing the passage of time.

the heart of inevitability is upon us.

words are unnecessary.
quiet breathing is all.

the nobility.
the bareness.
the intimation.
the envelopment.

elizabeth street garden

looking out your window,
this hushed city,
silhouetted against the sky,
unchanged,
whispers our existence
with defiant love.

what we have is a silent art,
or at least it deserves to be.
it deserves silent dignity.

our destinies are pivoting
across this elaborate universe
of what we've spent
a lifetime constructing.

this is our time,
and it has been
ennobled by kindness,
unearthed for all to see.

our disarmingly tender afternoon
among the trees and marble statutes
are all i need
because you
are the final breath
in this fading light.

truly alive

don't let every kiss feel
like half of what it should be.

don't be afraid of the ruin.
the ruin is the gift.

what is built after the destruction
is always more magnificent anyway.

life is still the leading cause of death,
and deep grief is still the natural part of love.

ache for that guarantee
and dream for that golden soul
with all the immensity
and richness of spirit.

do you want a stable life or a fragile one?

do you want the fading of experience into memory
or the memory of experience fading?

remember the moments.

remember the nights that stirred you most.

the sky will be more blue.

what was old will seem new again.

the hours will no longer vanish slowly.

and the impossibility
of being truly alive
will be yours
with nothing but brilliance
and bravery by your side.

the familiar stranger
(september 13, 2019)

the bittersweet
discovery of you
at this late hour,
and all the stories
you carry with you,
remind me again
that despair
is a terrible option,
and my slightly crestfallen soul
wants to dream of only you now.

with unending discovery
and a sense of anticipation,
i long to find delight
in everything, every day.

you remind me again
that it's still
the little things
that become the most memorable.

you remind me again
to treat the passing of seasons with nothing but reverence.

you remind me again
to befriend the world because it's all so much larger than us.

you remind me again
that it's the end of things that give them their true meaning.

you remind me again
to give of yourself with immense love and dedicated distinction.

you remind me again
to keep your needs simple and to never have aspirations
to be wealthy or famous or to stay young forever.

you remind me again
that if a little prosperity
comes your way,
then it should be shared with many.

you remind me again
that i want to be left

with only 2 things:

my bones bleaching under the brave sun
and the luminous reminiscence of our time together.

need

what we need is restoration
and then more rest.

it doesn't mean we have to
reject the world
or isolate ourselves,
but we need to
feel the lack.

because it's in the lack
where you will find the need.

it's the lingering dreams
that become your devotion.

it's the throat-catching beauty
that becomes your pain.

and it's the moments in between
that become your private truth.

don't lose this one right now.

healing

i see the lights of brooklyn
shimmering across the night sky,
and like great lovers
under the moon,
our souls unfurl
with unsparing romance.

writing these consolatory words for each other,

we know now what heals the soul
after medicine heals the body.

who i love the most

emma turns to me and says:

> *"daddy, you know who i love the most?*
> *grandpa and mia."*

why, emma?

> *"because grandpa is sick*
> *and mia is little."*

i stare at her face, astounded,
and every word she speaks
expands everything around me
with a supremely human touch
that is immeasurably redeeming.

the magnificence of this moment
will prevent the expiration of my heart
and stay with me, unfolding,
under subway grates and over rooftops,
in plain sight for all to see.

time

time is the most important thing of all.

time to think,
to dream,
to see,
to stand in front of you for hours,
for an entire day,
for days on end,
if possible.

the promise of you,
seeking solace after desolation,
and loving with an elegant vengeance
contained of grace and generosity.

you are the blur,
the unexplainable,
the in-between space where only love blooms,
and it blooms around the evocation
of our wandering spirits.

our recognition,
our rediscovery,
demands the closest possible attention.

you have mine.
you have me.

i am held in my own thoughts of you
and find myself
in your directed gaze,
but i am also taking account of it.

i am thinking about the distances
we have traveled to arrive here.

how these elegies
are for us now,
and how these words
and this love conjure eternities,
without hushed agonies,
without tempered regrets,
without wistful sorrows.

we push forward benevolently

and unflinchingly

as we take some of the torment of life
and make something wonderful out of it.

this time
it will be
quieter,
slower,
better.

toward her

read the books,
see the movies,
listen to the music,
look at everything in the museums,
and then turn and walk away from it all.

walk toward her.
she is there.

she is there like the sparkling sea,
and she will become
the captured heartbeat of your life.

untouched and touched madness

my stay upon earth
should have been brief,
but it looks like
i was misread
and misquoted.

i'm here still,
and so this is for you.

there is not much medicine
or the invented discipline of psychiatry
can do to alleviate
states of anguish,
damaged consciousness,
human horror.

at certain hours of the night,
never the day,
rapture arrives
to paint the landscape with purpose.

you whisper: *"hold me."*
i whisper: *"it will be ok."*

absolution.
consecration.
benediction.
respiration.

the true determination arrives,
followed by
sight,
hearing,
touch,
taste,
and smell.

the near-constant search for you has ended.

a last gasp has been given.

i'll burn for you
if you melt for me.

honesty

the flower fades,
and it extinguishes my last thoughts of you.

i want you to kiss me again
under the ever returning
fountain of stars.

so many are loved.
so few remain.

we try through
letters
and poems
and photographs
to capture what is
unknown to others
and what has eluded so many of us.

my soul is a bit faded
and timeworn,
but you have reclaimed and celebrated
all that is important
with your unceasing words to me
about the pleasures of ordinary devotion,
the persistence of admiration,
the obligation of gratitude,
the language of exaltation,
and the unquestioning strength of female honesty.

soho, new york

stretched out in perfect repose,
soho shows her splendor at night,
slowly revealing herself—
a special place and time
in its simplicity,
unassuming discretion,
history,
architecture,
romance.

inarguably, your beauty
enchants,
aches,
arrests,
informs.

time slows down a bit
when i walk these downtown streets,
and when i hold your hand.

it is simply the promise
that lies on the other side of all these sunsets.

the bridges of paris

under the bridges of paris with you,
and those metal padlocks
rendering these same bridges
too fragile to bear the weight of love.

and the understanding
of our hearts' portrait
allows this to become our resting place
before life's last moment.

you

on one of summer's final nights,
i undoubtedly think of you.

and on this day,
this week,
this month,
this year,
this decade,
this century,
this life

there is only you.

there was always, only you.

thank you.

sleep
(for emma and mia)

the emotion
of lying beside
my daughters
is usually such
that i don't sleep at all.

most of the night,
my affection and indulgence
haunt the hours
as i lie in darkness,
holding on to these threads of love
with serene companionship
and austere beauty,
and the wordlessness
and richness of its wondrous silence.

between me and the moon

without you here,
there is less to see.

i cast doubt on my achievements,
question my hopes,
judge my decisions,
interrogate my love,
criticize my life.

but what are still the same
are your eyes.

strange to think of you at this time,
but at least nothing now
stands between me, you, and the moon.

unwrap

life is change.
love is constancy.

the sorrows we suffer
keep us weary inside still,
but we accept the morning sun,
rising with affection,
unwrapping each other
in nights of sleep
as the stars sigh
on the most peaceful night of fall.

grasp my heart

slip your hand inside my shirt,
grasp my heart,
the one that beats
with a feeling
you will never be able to define.

not through
paintings
or drawings
or notebooks.

not through
monographs
or memoirs
or remembrances.

the truth stands before us now
as we rekindle the recognition
in one another
and remain remarkably bound
to our story and to our fate.

timing

when
we
were
good,

we
were
breathtaking.

spring street station
(*dawn chorus*)

riding the same subway
at the same time
on the same route
on the same nights
listening to the same song,
dreaming of the same you
all becoming as mindful as prayer.

walking out of the subway at spring street
and rising out of the earth,
where emotion comes together as i make my way
through these busy streets
to your apartment,
without noise,
but with a blue light
more radiant than
the space between knowing and unknowing,

and like the city shadows
that unfurl during the day
and are gone by night,
you are the one who eclipses all others.

putting the trembling kiss at ease

on gray afternoons,
as the violin weeps
and all that we hold
falls through our clutching hands.

we continue
doing hard,
undervalued work.

we continue
becoming enchanted
by common things.

we continue
with contentment to get nowhere,
taking each day as it comes.

we continue
knowing that the fact that
we exist at all
is already a miracle.

we continue
with our sense of wonder
serving as our only religion.

we continue
fully aware that greater wealth
never denotes greater character.

we continue
despite the greatest horrors
being committed on this planet.

we continue
keeping light-heartedness
as our antidote to life's solemnity.

we continue
as the corporations
and the governments
beholden to them,
choose profit over everything.

we continue
watching as winter
becomes ever more fragile.

we continue
with our triumphant discovery
that one person
makes the difference.

we continue
with our reverence
for the littlest things.

we continue
with our words and our music,
serving as the soundtrack of our lives.

we continue
with all the sadness
of the centuries
as we live with
the certainty of grief.

we continue
knowing we will lose
everything we love,
including our lives
and the lives of all we hold close.

we continue
by not allowing the violence
and brutality of the world
to erase our memory of kindness.

we continue
with the reverence
for the basic humanity
of being human.

we continue
by witnessing someone you love
discover something
you have long loved.

we continue
as we still misjudge

each other's inner worlds
based on outward appearances.

we continue
with messages of quiet contemplation
and the power of nonconformity.

we continue
knowing that
discord, suffering, and sorrow
are everywhere

we continue
knowing that the only reward
of all these words
has always been the words themselves.

we continue
even though the world
has not been trained in the disciplines
of love and compassion.

we continue
as we live between solitude
and communion.

we continue
as we search for the radiance
we live for.

we continue
through the art we make
and through the words we say.

we continue
as austere beauty
dances across the sky
and bends the arrow of time.

we continue
as the world banishes
our muses pushing them away
with our human gifts
of meaning and understanding.

we continue
as we let the achingly
cold nights hold us.

we continue
even through the final
ailing years of our life.

we continue
with our ancient affection
for the grand scale of the universe.

we continue
despite the internet,
the tv's, the cell phones,
the large trucks,
the loud music and the stock markets.

we continue
as the sunsets last
for hours in our minds.

we continue
on the hope of the
gentle-souled artist
who only wants to smell the flowers.

we continue
aware that each day
our human thoughts and feelings
don't want to stand still.

we continue
aware that the words we use
to comfort others matter.

we continue
knowing that if we are fortunate enough
to live a long life
our bodies will break down.

we continue
with nothing to offer
except eternal devotion,
and that is always enough.

we continue
knowing that love
is always within reach,
and that is always enough also.

we continue
with the promise
of rest and dreams.

we continue
by bearing the cost of forgiveness.

we continue
because we believe in something
bigger than ourselves.

we continue
with a willingness
to sacrifice one's interests
with profound humility
giving everyone
the benefit of some shared humanity.

we continue
as the earth takes 365 days
to go around the sun
creating silence
and allowing us to be still.

we continue
healing in our hurting world.

we continue
with a grace that allows
harmony into our souls.

we continue
living our life in person.

we continue
living through
the shortest days
and the longest nights of the year.

we continue
with that something
stirring in our hearts
from when we were children.

we continue
with our deepest reflections
as old as the human soul.

we continue
as we fall in love.

we continue
with our moments
of laughter, tenderness, and joy

we continue
with the hope
for a sense that we matter.

we continue
between our smallness
and the grandeur of this life.

and we continue
among the glimpses
of the unknown,
putting the trembling kiss at ease.

Postscript

some words that helped ...

Isabel the Butterfly
(A poem by Emma Silich, age 8, written February 4, 2021)

I am flying
with my gentle wings
under the sun
and above the trees.

I am flying
with my best friend
Isabel the Butterfly.

When I was resting,
someone tried to catch me
and hurt my wing,
so Isabel is helping me fly.

We are flying together
and enjoying how beautiful
the world looks from up here.

The Ginormous Heart
(A poem by Mia Silich, age 5, written February 25, 2021)

You know daddy
Your heart is ginormous
And when someone dies like 'GaGa' (grandpa)
It breaks wide open.

You may never see him again
Because I'm not sure people
live above the clouds,
But I know he is still an angel
watching over us somewhere.

I Walk the Beach with a Silent Friend
(A sonnet by Robert Christopher Silich, written in 1985, age 18)

I walk the beach with a silent friend,
As the sun paints my shadow across the sand.
Upon the shore my dreams do break and mend,
For the wind brings whispers from sea to land.

The sand behind is soft and warm.
The steps ahead await us, rough and cold.
The trail that follows bears our form,
While forward we lead, uncertain yet bold.

How far must we travel to where we must be?
Our footsteps, the answer, like the stitch of a seam,
Lead to the horizon we feel, but never can see.
The end to our walk, and the life of a dream.

We all walk the beach with our silent friends,
And in love we make a journey that never ends.

Shouts to the Angels Whether or Not They Listen
(A poem by Robert Christopher Silich, written in 1996, age 29)

Falling apart between two worlds
The worlds of the beautiful and the worlds of the ugly,
The well and the sick,
The rich and the poor,
The living and the dead,
Her world and mine.
To live in both is to live in neither.
To be absent from each but changing the course of both.

One world shines at the surface and is rotten at the core.
The other bleeds, is torn and withers,
Beneath which lies the greatest beauty of all,
But a beauty this life cannot see.

Do I see it ?
Am I arrogant enough to think I see both?
Do I dare live in both, touching both?

Sparkled eyes and the dull eyes of death,
a cold, quivering look,
The blank eyes of a caught fish, rotting shortly.
Dispose of the catch before the sun decays the flesh,
Zip the bag closed,
Leave and swim amongst the shining, smooth fish
Pretending that they never rot when caught,
They are special, they all believe.

I have to see this truth and return to the pretty people
Swimming in their beautiful ignorance.
They swim so beautifully and never see their brothers rotting on the ship's bow in this open boat.

Who is better off?
"One acquainted with the night," the famous poet writes.
It's not a gift. It's a curse, to see both.
It's a sin to try to tell the beautiful fish
what goes on above the sea.
They are smarter, the ones who never know.

Is that my advice?
If you see it once, nothing is ever the same.
Pray to never know.
Sleep then without fear,
And sleep you always shall without a tear.

Acknowledgements

I would like to thank my publisher, the Brooklyn Writers Press and Marina Aris for publishing this 3rd collection of poetry. Thank you, Marina, for your unwavering support, loyalty, trust, and our over 25-year friendship filled with kindness, tenderness, and understanding.

I would like to thank my editor, Judi Heidel, for her always gentle approach and touch to my words. Thank you, Judi.

And I would like to thank:

My daughters, Emma and Mia — words are simply never enough. I love you more than anything — to the moon and back 100 million times.

Emma, thank you for writing these words on my sneaker:

"I am always with you, Love Emma"
November 15, 2021

And Mia, thank you for your words when you said:

"Daddy, can I tell you a secret?
You are a flower, and you will always have my heart."
September 2, 2021

My dad, Robert J. Silich (October 10, 1941 — October 28, 2020)
I miss you more each day and feel your presence in everything I do. Thank you. I love you. Thank you for your words:

"You always make me proud. You are my greatest gift.
No words can express the depth of my love for you."
October 11, 2006

My mom, Dianne Silich — my hero. My beautiful hero. I love you. The letter you sent me 36 years ago, I keep with me still:

"I love you and I'm always proud of you, perhaps more than anyone because you have always had to work harder and overcome more obstacles than anyone I know. You have always made us proud, and you fill us all with your goodness. I love you; you are a part of me. I'll be thinking of you and wishing you only happiness. All my love forever." February 9, 1986

My brother, Robert C. Silich — the only person I have ever looked up to and the only true gentleman I know. Thank you for inspiring and sustaining me. I love you. And thank you for your words:

"You figured it out so much sooner than I did, about how it all really is. You are always my first thought with good news and even not so good news. We are two of a kind, out of 6.77 billion people. We share the exact same DNA and I stay quiet more often than not when you finish my sentences — which happens more now than ever. I love you so much, my brother, the nicest guy I know." April 30, 2009

My grandmother, Greta Silich (April 3, 1915 – February 17, 2007)
I miss you Nana and thank you for the reminder you sent me:

"Stephan, dear, always remember that love knows no limit." February 2, 1985

My former teacher and mentor, Fr. David Ciancimino, SJ — thank you for the encouraging words you sent me:

"Steve, you have a very special gift with words, so please keep writing. I think you will learn in time that life is a series of some good and some not so good experiences. Our only hope is that through these experiences we can come to know ourselves better and do better for ourselves and for others — especially for those who love us so deeply." July 4, 1984

For the others — the very few others — you know who you are, and I thank you for sharing art and air with me, and for allowing the wonder of life to always prevail, despite it all.

About the Author

"Silich slips effortlessly into a long tradition of New York poets from Whitman to Frank O'Hara and his poems are a delight."

– KIRKUS REVIEWS

Stephan Silich is an award-winning writer and poet. His second collection, 'tonight is the longest night of them all' was a finalist in the 2021 Next Generation Independent Book Awards. His first collection, 'the silence between what i think and what i say' released in 2018 also received rave reviews.

Silich continues to write daily and has several more collections in the works. He lives in Manhattan and East Hampton with his two daughters, Emma and Mia.

Connect with Stephan on Instagram @stephan_silich

Thank You for Reading
Putting The Trembling Kiss at Ease

If you enjoyed this book, please consider leaving a
short review on Goodreads or your platform of choice.

Reviews help both readers and writers.
They are an easy say to support good work and help to
encourage the continued release of quality content.

Want the latest from the Brooklyn Writers Press?

Browse our complete catalog.
brooklynwriterspress.com

www.ingramcontent.com/pod-product-compliance
Lightning Source LLC
Chambersburg PA
CBHW070136080526
44586CB00015B/1715

PRAISE FOR STEPHAN SILICH'S POETRY COLLECTIONS

"Stephan's beautiful poetry collections are stunning and comforting to hold. The covers are breathtaking. What a beautiful way to capture his photography and share it with his readers. In reading *The Silence Between What I Think and What I Say* I noticed his verses and reflections are incredibly endearing and touching. What a gifted writer. I am savoring every poem I read. It is an honor to read his work and take a pause with his poetic wisdom. I find myself reading his words from the perspective of a father raising two girls, like mine did. To read from his point of view has been very cathartic."

SOPHIA DEV
Author of *'Grit in Her Veins, Grace in Her Soul'*

"I love the slices of life as short poems, they're so intimate and interesting. Stephan's collections are moving… especially his words on life, death, and New York. I've never read a poetry book, a few poems yes, but never a collection straight through. I think artists connect because they suffer more deeply than others and because they feel more deeply than others. Maybe this is why I trust artists, because they feel so much more than others feel. Stephan is an artist with words."

OZ VANROSEN
Artist

"Stephan's collections are wonderful to read, especially at night. They are soothing and really make one go *Aha!* as the words are what we all wish to express so eloquently."

NINA FORD RICHTER

"Stephan's poems are achingly beautiful."

CLEOPATRA FERNHILL

"I started reading *The Silence Between What I Think and What I Say* and it moved me to tears. The one that really got to me was 'for Alan.' Stephan's poems are so honest, beautiful, and captivating. He really knows how to write from the heart. He has reinvigorated my passion for poetry. He speaks to the human experience and has such a beautiful outlook on life and living in New York City…Stephan's poetry makes me feel like I'm seeing into his soul. His poetry is so beautiful, and I can tell he has a deep and profound connection to each piece I've read. I find his writing, so honest, and visceral."

HANNAH FLAM

"Stephan has written fabulous books of poetry. I don't know how he thinks of these beautiful ideas, but I love reading them. His poetry makes my heart and soul happy."

TONIA GORDON

"Stephan's poetry is exquisite. It's spiritual, soulful, and simply beautiful. I have such moments of tranquility reading his writing. I recently read his poem '50 things I've learned in 50 years' and can only think of how very fortunate his daughters are to have such a wise dad. I'm relating these poems to my own life, and all I can feel is awe…for the moments of tranquility felt reading his work."

JOYCE REIMER

"Stephan's collections are spectacular. I love his writing. Can't wait for the next one."

CAROLYN SWEETAPPLE

"Stephan's work is the summation of a life lived without regret."

DELISA GAINES

"Stephan's words are always inspiring."

KAREN ANN

"Stephan's poems resonate with me to such a degree I can feel my heart expand. His poems are beautiful expressions."

DR. JAMIE HESKETT

"After reading Stephan's poems, I share a moment with my heart."

ALLAN WEIDENBAUM

"Stephan has an angelic soul, and his transparency is so real and relatable. All of it is simply moving. Stephan's words have inspired me to do things I postponed for years."

ERICA CALIA KASTELL

"I'm a deep thinker, so many of Stephan's words resonate with me. He is extremely talented. His collections are even more beautiful in printed form. I read through a bunch of passages, hoping I could tell him, which was my favorite, but every poem I read was my new favorite! I am forever grateful."

MARYANN LANGER

"After I read Stephan's poetry, I can go to sleep in peace with his beautiful words."

RAPHAEL VITRAT

"Stephan is a fabulous poet who touches everyone's heart. He is such a rare talent. All his words are so moving and poignant."

CAROL NOBBS

"Stephan's words are so carefully and thoughtfully written-with love. I would wait a lifetime for his words. He is such an incredibly open, honest person with so much love to share. I love all the family stories and memories. I can see the words come to life. All his words are beautiful and romantic. I live reading his words, and so glad I found his collections. He is gifted with so much talent."

LEAH VITALE

"Stephan's words are like feathers sensationally touching the heart."

HELEN NASRA

"I read Stephan's poetry often. I select a page at random, and his words always resonate with me. I keep his collections on my desk at work, and they always give my brain some space to breathe. They are beautiful."

KRISTINE GARLISI

"Stephan's authenticity and openness shines through on every page. I particularly related to his poems about fatherhood. I love how each poem tells a story and offers important life advice. His words have a genuine and profound impact that is both refreshing and inspiring. I consider his first two collections literary masterpieces and look forward to delving deeper into his work. I will cherish his books forever."

DR. ROBERT SPENCER

"Stephan's collections have inspired me in unimaginable ways."

DR. DAVID LANGER

"Stephan's poetry is outstanding. Every time I read his words; uninvited tears fall."

PEDJMAN MOHAMMADI
Artist

"I'm breathless. I'm in awe. I'm full of joy. I'm heartbroken. I'm full of tears. I lie awake at night thinking of Stephan's poems. I go about my day and have his words with me. It truly is a joy to look inside his soul."

AGGI TONGA

"One of my favorites of Stephan's poems is '*50 things I've learned in 50 years.*' I really enjoy his writing style because of how deeply it connects and made me feel like we need to appreciate and be grateful for all the blessings and little things we take for granted in life. Stephan's postscripts, 'A Father's Thoughts' and acknowledgments are such warm and beautiful ways to end a book."

ADAM HENRY

"I love Stephan's collections. When I read his work, I am home. His poetry has given me back something I lost, which now I have found again. I'm so looking forward to reading his next collection and the one after that. Stephan made the right decision to share his poetry with the world. There are a lot of people out there who need to know they're not alone, and his poems can help them know that. His writing is like a best friend talking to you and telling you it's okay if you fail or if your relationship didn't work out, tomorrow is a new day. There is something for everyone in some time or period in their life. Stephan has captured our hurt as well as his own, and that is how we all know we are not alone and that life isn't perfect, but to remember love, and family, and loving memories are with you always no matter how short-lived."

CHRISTINE HOLLISTER

"I absolutely loved '*Putting The Trembling Kiss at Ease*' just as I loved Stephan's prior two collections. His presence is oddly quiet in his work, almost like he is invisible, a ghost in his own stories, yet writing thoughtfully and with a big heart, as if he was standing next to the last word of every sentence in each poem."

JENNIFER FONTAO

"I am in love with Stephan's heart, his words, his way of thinking, and his experiences. We never know who is feeling the same things we are feeling and going through the same experiences we are with the same intensity. I am in awe of his poetry. I can't put his books down. When I read his poems, I feel I am on a rollercoaster of emotions, and I am living my own life all over again as I read. Stephan shares his experiences with his readers so selflessly. He has a heart of gold."

PAMELA FLORES

"I read Stephan's book *'Putting The Trembling Kiss at Ease.'* I read every page while sitting mesmerized on a small island in the Swedish West Coast Archipelago. The poems are so immensely touching. Stephan's way of using words is a true art. And what's not written leaves me wondering in the way art should leave a space for personal reflections and interpretations. The design of the book is beautiful in so many ways. The cover has a most wonderful texture and so have the pages, kind of accompanying the softness of the message. Stephan's cover photography with the shadows is stunning. Congratulations to Stephan and to the rest of the world for having this treasure to pass on from generation to generation."

EVA CHRISTINA NIELSEN,
"Author Of Oclust"

"Stephan's words gently guide me toward a more thoughtful, balanced, and compassionate way of living with self-worth and kindness to others."

DARIA TELEGIN

"I cannot recommend *'The Silence Between What I Think and What I Say'* enough. All the beautiful words, thoughts, and stories contained within it I return to over-and-over again, especially when I feel beaten down by the brutality of the world. Stephan is a beacon of light, reminding us of what really matters. His poetry helped me immensely and I have no doubt it touches many others just as deeply. Stephan's words make the world a little bit more beautiful. I always feel a little less lonely and a lot more hopeful because there are so many amazing, beautiful humans out there fumbling their way through life; being vulnerable is hard and necessary. Words have the power to heal, and Stephan's poetry heals."

JENNIFER BENTLEY

"I highly recommend Stephan's poetry. I have the first three collections, and his words give us all a chance to think, feel, and see a new way of life."

DALIA FORMAN